The Key to My Heart

Art by GAY TALBOTT BOASSY

HARVEST HOUSE PUBLISHERS
Eugene, Oregon

The Key to My Heart

Text Copyright © 2000 Harvest House Publishers
Eugene, Oregon 97402

ISBN 0-7369-0098-5

Artwork designs are reproduced under license from © Arts Uniq'®, Inc., Cookeville, TN and may not be reproduced without permission. For information regarding art prints featured in this book, please contact:

     Arts Uniq'
     P.O. Box 3085
     Cookeville, TN 38502
     800-223-5020

Design and production by Garborg Design Works

Harvest House Publishers has made every effort to trace the ownership of all poems and quotes. In the event of a question arising from the use of a poem or quote, we regret any error made and will be pleased to make the necessary correction in future editions of this book.

Scripture quotations are taken from the Holy Bible, New International Version®, Copyright © 1973, 1978, 1984 by the International Bible Society. Used by permission of Zondervan Publishing House.

00 01 02 03 04 05 06 07 08 09 /PP/ 10 9 8 7 6 5 4 3 2 1

*Smile, it is the key that fits the
lock of everybody's heart.*

ANTHONY J. D'ANGELO

A hug warms the soul and
places a smile in the heart.

Author Unknown

The cheerful heart has a continual feast.

The Book of Proverbs

The most wonderful of all
things in life, I believe,
is the discovery of another
human being with whom
one's relationship has a
glowing depth, beauty, and
joy as the years increase.

SIR HUGH WALPOLE

5

A good
friend
is hard
to find,
hard to
lose, and
impossible
to forget.

*Lyndsey
Boucherle*

*There is no distance too
far between friends,
for friendship gives
wings to the heart.*

KATHY KAY BENUDIZ

You can't wrap love in a box,
but you can wrap a person in a hug!

Author Unknown

A hug is a handshake from the heart.

Author Unknown

Let your heart guide you.
It whispers, so listen closely.

AUTHOR UNKNOWN

©Gay Talbott-Boassy

It is not the level of prosperity
that makes for happiness
but the kinship
of heart to heart.

Alexandr Solzhenitsyn

Let love and
faithfulness
never leave you...
write them
on the tablet
of your heart.

The Book of Proverbs

11

My Teddy was there when I had
no friends to play with, no one to
talk to, no one to share my little
woes or my big joys. He looked
constant and was constant. He
never aged, no matter how tat-
tered he became. His smell was
the smell of my years as a boy, and
he alone knew everything. Now,
when I see him on the shelf, he is
like my flesh and my soul—older,
worn, but still full of happiness.

Robert Kunciov

*Even though
there is a rip in
your teddy bear,
his love will not
fall out.*

EVE FRANCES
GIGLIOTTI

HANDLE WITH CARE

Teddy Bear hugs are like chocolate:
You can never get enough.

Author Unknown

13

The most beautiful discovery true
friends make is that they can
grow separately without
growing apart.

Elisabeth Foley

It is the heart that makes a
man rich. He is rich
according to what he is, not
according to what he has.

HENRY WARD BEECHER

A best friend's treasure
Is her best friend's heart
I knew we'd become friends
From the very start.

Author Unknown

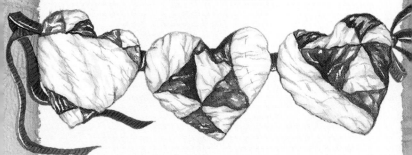

*How rare and wonderful
is that flash of a moment
when we realize we
have discovered a friend.*

WILLIAM ROTSLER

The happiest moments my heart knows are those in which it is pouring forth its affections to a few esteemed characters.

Thomas Jefferson

I keep my friends as misers do their treasure, because, of all the things granted us by wisdom, none is greater or better than friendship.

PIETRO ARETINO

A part of you has grown in me, together forever we shall be, never apart, maybe in distance, but not in heart.

AUTHOR UNKNOWN

© Gay Talbott Boassy

**A happy heart
makes the
face cheerful.**

The Book of Proverbs

*Kindness is the golden key that
unlocks the hearts of others.*

AUTHOR UNKNOWN

Where your pleasure is, there is your treasure: where your treasure, there your heart; where your heart, there your happiness.

Augustine

**To be loved is
to live forever in
someone's heart.**

Author Unknown

*Listen and attend with
the ear of your heart.*

SAINT BENEDICT

23

LITTLE LITTLE BEARS
LITTLE LITTLE MEN
LITTLE WOMEN

24

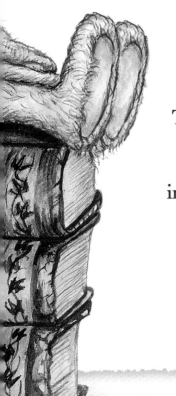

Love is the language our hearts use to speak to one another. For you, my dear, my heart sings.

AMANDA R. BYRD

The best and most
beautiful things
in the world cannot
be seen, nor
touched...but are
felt in the heart.

Helen Keller

*I am beginning to learn
that it is the sweet, simple
things of life which are
the real ones after all.*

LAURA INGALLS WILDER

Friendships are what our dreams are made of.
We hold onto each other with its binding love.
We stand close to each other, hand in hand,
Showing each other we understand.
Some friends may come and go,
But you are the truest friend I know.

Elsa Maxwell

BIRD SEED

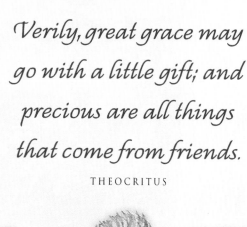

Verily, great grace may
go with a little gift; and
precious are all things
that come from friends.

THEOCRITUS

Life is short and we have never too
much time for gladdening the hearts of
those who are traveling...with us. Oh be
swift to love, make haste to be kind.

Henri-Frederic Amiel

There can be no happiness equal to the joy of finding a heart that understands.

Victor Robinson

Every friend I have ever
loved has contributed
to my happiness, strength,
and understanding.
A part of them
remains in me.

HELEN KELLER

31

Love is that condition in which
the happiness of another
person is essential to your own.

Robert Heinlein

*Making a friend just
takes a moment,
but being a friend
takes a lifetime.*

AUTHOR UNKNOWN

Friendship is...
Conversations and jokes together,
The mutual rendering of good services,
The reading together of sweetly phrased books,
The sharing of nonsense and mutual attentions.

Author Unknown

34

Nature has no love for solitude,
And always leans, as it were,
On some support;
And the sweetest support is found
In the most intimate friendship.

Cicero

Love is but the discovery
of ourselves in others, and the
delight in the recognition.

ALEXANDER SMITH

*One word frees us of
all the weight and pain
in life. That word is love.*

SOPHOCLES

**A friend is
someone who
understands
your past,
believes in
your future,
and accepts
you today
just the way
you are.**

*Robert Louis
Stevenson*

© Gay Talbott Boassy

The good
man brings
good things
out of the good
stored up in
his heart.

The Book of Luke

I like not only to be loved,
but to be told that I am loved.

GEORGE ELIOT

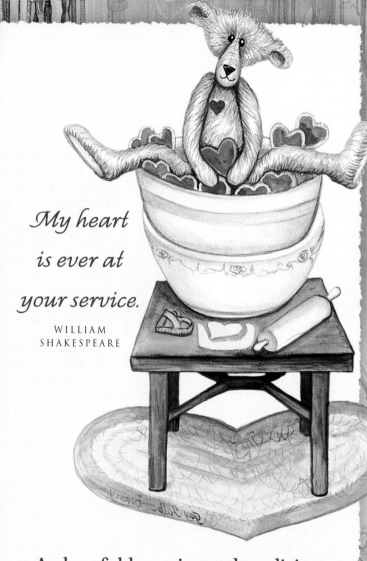

My heart is ever at your service.

WILLIAM SHAKESPEARE

A cheerful heart is good medicine.

The Book of Proverbs

40

For memory has painted this perfect day

With colors that never fade,

And we find at the end of a perfect day

The soul of a friend we've made.

Carrie Jacobs Bond

A friend is somebody you want to be around when you feel like being by yourself.

BARBARA BURROW

Happiness isn't the easiest thing to find, but one place you're guaranteed to find it is in a friend's smile.

Allison Poler

A friend is what the heart needs all the time.

Henry Van Dyke

© Gay Talbott Boassy

What brings joy
to the heart is not
so much the
friend's gift as the
friend's love.

*Saint Alfred
of Rievaulx*

A friend is someone who

reaches for your hand ... but

touches your heart.

UNKNOWN

A cheerful
look brings
joy to the
heart.

*The Book of
Proverbs*

46

A loving heart is the truest wisdom.

Charles Dickens

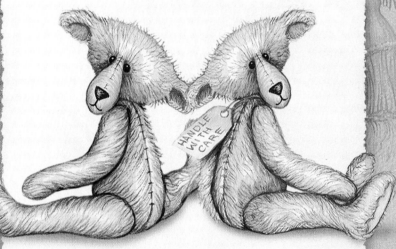

Our sweetest experiences of affection are meant to point us to that realm which is the real and endless home of the heart.

Henry Ward Beecher

There is a treasure chest inside
of me filled with thoughts
of you. In my quiet moments
I open it and cherish again
the friendship we share.

AUTHOR UNKNOWN

48